Grammar for Writers & Bloggers

Amber Roshay
Edited by Melissa Uhles

ABOUT YOUR INSTRUCTORS

We (Melissa and Amber) met eons ago in undergraduate school. Our lives have taken us to different cities over the years, but three things have kept us connected—writing, motherhood, and commiserating about our math-minded husbands.

In 2016 we co-wrote a romance novel together. After realizing we enjoyed collaborating and helping other parents and writers, we launched Pen and Parent to share our journey and inspire a like-minded tribe.

I (this is Amber) have more than 10 years' experience as an English instructor. I'm the author of three novels. I have an MFA in Creative Writing from The California College of the Arts. My writing has been featured in Motherly, *The Write Life, WOW! Women on Writing*, Business Insider, and more. I'm a mom of two under three.

I (this is Melissa) have authored four novels, a children's picture book, and recently a short film. I've been published online at *The Oregonian, The Pennyhoarder, Momastery, Red Tricycle, Rage Against the Minivan,* and more. I'm a mom of one sweet fourth grader.

"Good writing consists of mastering the fundamentals (vocabulary, grammar, the elements of style) and then filling the third level of your toolbox with the right instruments." - Stephen King

Most people zone out when it comes to grammar. The word alone brings on a yawn and eyelids begin to droop. But bloggers need to know how to edit their writing, not only to work with an editor but to craft consistent, high-quality writing that competes.

Perhaps you've read our other books, **Write Compelling Content or How to Make a Living as a Writer** and realized that your editing and grammar skills needed polish, or perhaps you want to become an expert grammarian.

Regardless, this refresher will tighten your blogging prose, grammar skills, and syntax knowledge. There are writing exercises so that you can practice! Grab a pen and paper or set up near your laptop.

Grammar for Writers & Bloggers includes two sections.

Section 1 - *How to Improve Your Grammar Immediately*
Section 2 - *Top Grammar Mistakes Even Professional Writers and Bloggers Make*

There is also a bonus at the end.

By the end of this book, you will have accomplished the following (heck, yeah):

Gained grammar confidence

Identified the most common grammar errors

Fixed the most common grammar errors

Applied your new skills to your own writing

Written 1,000 words

TABLE OF CONTENTS

Section 1 - How to Improve Your Grammar Immediately

Get Rid of Adverbs
Make Verbs Stronger
Get Rid of the Word That
Create Sentence Variety
Use Parallel Structure
Ditch the Passive
Lose there is/are
Remove Redundancies
Replace Stuffy Words with Simpler Ones
Use Synonyms

Section 2 - Top Grammar Mistakes Even Professional Writers and Bloggers Make

Possessives
Subject-Verb Agreement
Fragments
Punctuation
Run-On Sentences
Their vs. There vs. They're
Vague Pronoun Reference
Misplaced or Dangling Modifier

Bonuses
Identify Your Tells

SECTION 1: How to Improve Your Grammar Immediately

Get Rid of the Adverbs

I secretly loved adverbs. I found that using one to emphasize a key point fits how I speak so this would translate into my writing. But modifiers aren't needed, most of the time or I should say, they are hated by many writers. Almost every book published about the craft of writing will tell you to abolish them.

Adverbs tell the reader *how, how much, how often*, or *where* something is/was done.

The sign for an adverb is that it ends -ly, for example, *usually, honestly, boldly, really, very*, and so on.

But adverbs don't always end in -ly. Some of these adverbs include: *most, never, often, only*, and so on.

Adverbs usually modify verbs, but they can also modify adjectives. I use the word "modify" to mean to add more information to the verb or adjective.

Let's Look at Two Examples of Adverb Usage.

In which sentence is the adverb modifying the verb, and in

which one is it modifying the adjective?

The dog <u>really</u> needs to stop chewing the kids' toys.

The color of the dog's eyes is <u>really</u> brown.
In the first sentence, "really" is modifying the verb "needs."
In the second sentence, "really" is modifying the adjective "brown."

But do we "really" need "really" in the above sentences? In sentence one, if we take out "really" to leave, "The dog needs to stop chewing the kid's toys," the sentence is stronger.

Yet, if this sentence came about in a conversation about getting rid of the dog, really might need to emphasize if he "really" doesn't stop chewing the toys, I'm going to get rid of him.

However, this doesn't mean that you shouldn't ever use adverbs. In fact, adverbs can make your sentences precise and nuanced. But when you have lots of them, it weakens the writing.

So, you need to evaluate every adverb and ask yourself if it's required. If it isn't, say a fond goodbye.

Let's look at another example:

Maria *tightly* held onto her son's squirming hand, trying *desperately* to put off the much-thought about moment of *quickly* dropping him off at preschool for the first time.

In this sentence, we have a few adverbs and words that aren't needed. I'm tempted to keep tightly, but I know we don't need it. Based on the context, of course, Maria's holding her son's hand tightly.

We can also delete desperately. And much thought about moment in this sentence is confusing. Quickly isn't necessary in the sentence, and it distracts from the moment.

Rewriting this sentence might look something like this:

Maria gripped her son's hand, wanting to avoid dropping him off at preschool for the first time.

We went from 28 words to 17 by removing the adverbs, unnecessary phrasing and upgrading our verbs.

The reasons adverbs hurt your writing is because <u>they can be redundant</u>, <u>weaken your verbs</u>, and <u>if you already have an adjective, you don't need a modifier</u>.

Another Example

She judiciously snarked meanly. "You've got to be kidding. I really hate it when you look at me so wantonly." Jose snuck a quick look at her snarling face, wondering how he could have ever loved her so grandly.

First of all, I'm unsure what *judiciously snarked meanly* means. Judiciously means prudence, so one snaps with mean prudence? Confusing.

Next, *wantonly* is for romance novels set in the 1930s. We can combine "snuck a quick look" with a more impactful verb like *peaked*. And do we really need so *grandly* when we talk about loving someone?

Jose peaked at her angry face, wondering how he could have ever loved her. "You've got to be kidding," she said. "I really hate it when you look at me with such dove eyes."

I'm not happy with dove eyes, but for now, we'll keep it. I replaced the verb *snarked* with *said* because using snappy verbs can be distracting when all you really need is *says* or *said* in dialogue. I changed the sentences around for clarity. Beginning with Jose peaking a look makes her comment clearer.

Practice Exercise

Instructions: Describe a busy scene in a daycare center, a visit to the pediatrician, dance recital, or playground without using adverbs or adjectives. Write 3-4 paragraphs describing this scene.

Remember that nouns and verbs are your friends.

Instructions: Now that you've written 3-4 paragraphs without adverbs and adjectives go back and add adjectives and adverbs to the paragraphs. Which sentences do you like better?

Final Exercise: Ask yourself, did you find this exercise easy or difficult? Why?

Now, go back to a blog post or article you've written and review. Highlight all the adverbs, so they stand out. Do you need them? Do they make your writing stronger? If not, get rid of the -lys.

Make Your Verbs Stronger

Since we know that the weak adverb has been ostracized, you need to have stronger
verbs to compensate. Strong verbs allow readers to visualize the story and draw them into your writing.

Saying "he went to the store" is different from "he strolled to the store" or "he skipped to the store."

When it comes to verbs, I think of the Harry Potter books by J.K. Rowling. She uses verbs like groaned, snapped, barked, and complained. If you read her writing, her verb choices jump off of the page. In fact, reading them is a joy. However, my writing mentor in college hated Rowling's use of the verb choices for dialogue. He insisted using *said* for dialogue tags was the perfect choice. In the end, know the rules; then you can break them.

Check out these opening lines and how strong verbs create power.

"The night breathed through the apartment like a dark animal."
Reckless by Cornelia Funke

"It was the day my grandmother exploded.
The Crow Road by Iain M. Banks

Example 1: The man was walking on the street. *Weak verb choice*

The man strode on the street. *Strong verb choice*

Example 2: Darcy was smiling derisively as she walked. *Weak verb choice*

Darcy snickered as she walked. *Strong verb choice*

Example 3: She was thinking what all the fuss was about when she came upon a man in a back felt hat and everything came together in one sizzling pop.

She was musing about all the fuss when she stumbled upon a man wearing a black felt hat, making the reason clear as day.

We changed *thinking* to *musing* and *came upon* to *stumble*. We also changed the end of the sentence for clarity.

Here are a few fun *ing* verbs to try:
Pacing, biting, muttering, lunging, weeping, flinching, scrambling, huddling, scowling, jeering

Exercise 1: Write a paragraph using the five verbs below.

Treasured, stormed, berated, lurked, and grasped.

Exercise 2: Review a blog post or article you've written. Are the verbs strong or weak? What verb can you use to replace them? What one-word verb can you exchange for two or more words?

Get Rid of "That"

Now, who doesn't love a little this and that?

Well, like adverbs "that" isn't always necessary. Removing the relative pronoun makes your sentences shorter and clearer, but also more informal. Removing "that" is also more common in speech than in writing but removing them will add clarity to your blog posts.

Before we dive into removing "that" from your writing, it's essential to review the grammar of relative pronouns and how they work in a sentence.

This, *that*, *who*, *what*, *where*, and *why* are relative pronouns. Relative pronouns appear in adjective clauses and noun clauses.

Things to Know About Adjective and Noun Clauses

It begins with a relative pronoun (this, that, who, what, where & why)

It has a noun and a verb.

It will tell us something about the noun.

The relative pronoun can be omitted (this is what you should do with your writing, if possible).

Adjective and Noun Clauses Examples

Thomas loves **that** you've decided to come tomorrow.

I truly think that <u>he'll love **that** you've decided to come tomorrow.</u>

I know a person **that** <u>can help you.</u>

I want a car **that** <u>gets good gas mileage.</u>

In all the examples above, the adjective clauses begin with "that," has a noun and a verb, and tells us something about the noun.

Two of the examples "that" can be omitted. What are they?

Yes, numbers one and two. Most of the time, you know the answer because it doesn't sound right without "that" in the sentence. But one way to know for sure is to look at what precedes "that" in the sentence. If a verb comes before "that," then you can usually remove it. I say "usually" because there are exceptions. If a noun precedes "that," then you can't omit it.

Thomas loves you've decided to come tomorrow. "That," in the original sentence, comes after the verb "loves," making it possible to omit "that."

I truly think he'll love you've decided to come tomorrow. "That," in the original sentence, comes after the verb "think," making it possible to omit "that."

In sentences three and four, "that" comes after nouns (person and car), making the relative pronoun necessary in the sentence.

Have I overwhelmed you with all this grammar? I hope not. I find that knowing the rules makes you a better writer because knowledge takes the guesswork out.

Exercise 1: Review an article or blog post you've written and remove any unnecessary "thats."

Sentence Variety

In any good piece of writing, sentence variety is essential. If you repeat the same kind of sentence over and over again, your writing is annoying and childish. You need to vary the style and length of your sentences to make your writing more exciting and professional.

Let's review the paragraph below. Are the sentences varied?

I went to the bank. I saw the man in the bank. He looked at me and smiled. We locked eyes. I nodded my head, and he followed. We went to the cafe close by. We ordered coffee in silence. The day had arrived.

Not really. Most of the sentences have a subject, verb, and object only.

I *went* to the <u>bank</u>. "I" is the subject, "went" is the verb, and "bank" is the object.

The conjunction "and" was used twice. So, the writing in the paragraph above relies mostly on simple sentences and compound sentences using "and."

Now, let's add some variety.

I stepped into the bank with anticipation. I scanned the crowd to find the man who gazed at me and smiled. As we locked eyes, I nodded my head, and he followed me out of the bank to a cafe close by. We ordered coffee. The day had arrived.

We now have more sentence variety in the paragraph above, combining two simple sentences with the relative pronoun "who" and beginning one sentence with the connecting phrase, "As we locked eyes."

To help you practice using varied sentence structure, let's review three common types of sentences.

Simple Sentence

All you need to create a simple sentence is a subject and a verb. You can also have an object.

I went to the bank.
Tamara stared at the man.
The cat jumped from the counter.

A simple sentence is a complete sentence that can stand on its own without any other information added.

Compound Sentence

To create a compound sentence, you will connect two simple sentences or two or more independent clauses with a conjunction, such as "and."

When I was in school, the FANBOYS acronym was a popular teaching tool to help us memorize conjunctions.

F: For
A: And
N: Nor
B: But
O: Or
Y: Yet
S: So

I went to the store, **and** then I drove home.

I would love to go to the store and the bank, **but** I need to see a man about a dog.

Tamara wasn't sure about coming, **so** she headed over to the bar to get a drink first.

Complex Sentence

A complex sentence is one simple sentence or independent clause and one dependent clause.

An independent clause is a sentence that can stand on its own, meaning you don't need any other information for it to be understood. While a dependent clause may have a subject and verb, it can't be entirely understood by itself. The dependent clause needs an independent clause for complete understanding. I like to think of it as a marriage.

Complex Sentence Examples

Note: the dependent clauses are underlined.

<u>While I devoured my book</u>, my cat licked my feet.

<u>Because she's tired</u>, Katie can't come for a sleepover.

She became angry <u>after she discovered him with another woman</u>.

I have to see this movie <u>since my sister's the central star</u>.

In the examples above, each sentence has an independent clause and a dependent clause. The dependent clause begins with a connecting word such as *while*, *after*, and *since*.

You can also switch the dependent and independent clause in the sentences.

My cat licked my feet while I devoured my book.

Katie can't come for a sleepover because she's tired.

After she discovered him with another woman, she became angry.

Since my sister's the central star, I have to see this movie.

When the sentence begins the dependent clause, there will be a comma at the end, right before the independent clause.

While I devoured my **book, my** cat licked my feet.

If the sentence begins with the independent clause, you won't use a comma to divide the two clauses.

She became angry <u>after she discovered him with another woman</u>.

Exercise 1: Write a paragraph using two simple sentences, one compound sentence and two complex sentences.

Exercise 2: Review a blog post or article you've written to make sure you have sentence variety. Make the necessary changes.

Lack of Parallel Structure

Parallel structure (parallelism) is when you create repetition in your sentence using a chosen grammatical form. By making similar ideas or comparisons with the same grammatical structure, you give them equal importance. Parallelism also creates a nice rhythm and structure to your sentences, giving them a professional polish.

The usual way to create a parallel structure is through the use of conjunctions, such as "and" or "or." Parallelism can happen in any part of the sentence.

Using a Gerund (ing form of the word)

I love swimm**ing**, runn**ing**, and hik**ing**. *Parallel Structure*
I love swimm**ing**, runn**ing**, and **to hike**. *NOT Parallel Structure*

Note: it's important not to mix parallel structures.

Using an Infinitive

I love **to swim**, **to run**, and **to hike**. *Parallel Structure*

I love **to swim,** runn**ing,** and **to hike**. *NOT Parallel Structure*

Clauses

I thought **that there would be food**, **plenty of drinks**, and **beautiful girls**.
NOT Parallel Structure

Note: Although for a stronger sentence removing the *that there* in the clauses is a smarter choice.

I thought **that there would be food**, **that there would be drinks**, and **that there would be girls**. *Parallel Structure*

Balance of Words in a List

The lessons in the course are **vocabulary acquisition, grammatical structure,** and **communicative activities**.
Parallel Structure

The lessons in the course are **learning vocabulary acquisition, grammatical forms and structure,** and **communicative activities**. *NOT Parallel Structure*

Matching Headers

In an article or blog post, headers are standard. Headers need to use parallel structure. They also need to be easy to scan.

The mistake I see most often is not using verbs - or using different verb forms--in some points of lists.

For example:

Blog Title: How to Holiday Shop on a Budget

Header 1: Make a List
Header 2: Budget
Header 3: Watching for Sales Months in Advance

NOT Parallel Structure

Note: All the headers are three words and begin with an imperative verb.

Blog Title: How to Holiday Shop on a Budget

Header 1: Make a List
Header 2: Create a Budget
Header 3: Watch for Sales

Parallel Structure

Exercise: Review your article. Begin by looking at the language around "and" and "or." Do you use parallel structure? Read your article out loud to hear the rhythm and style. What doesn't flow? Make the necessary changes.

Ditch the Passive

I remember my high school English teacher speaking of the "passive" as if she had found it smeared on the bottom of her shoe. The passive has always gotten a bad rap. Well, until you reach college and suddenly your English teacher assigns an academic essay and asks you to include passive language when needed. And you realize that the passive construction increases your word count.

So, what is it, *active* or *passive*? Well, **active** of course.

However, passive language is sometimes used in writing academic papers, describing important processes, and highlighting essential actions. Otherwise, remove the pesky passive construction from your writing.

Passive Grammatical Structure

Form of the "to be" verb + past participle

I **was rushed** through the assignment by my teacher. *Passive*
The teacher **rushed** me through the assignment. *Active*

The rat **was caught** by the trap. *Passive*
The trap **caught** the rat. *Active*

In a passive sentence, the object of the action is at the beginning of the sentence, and the subject is at the end.

The rat **was caught** by the trap. *Passive*

The rat is the object of the action (was caught) and the subject is the trap, which did the catching. To make the sentence active switch the subject and object of the action in the sentence.

The trap **caught** the rat. *Active*

Once you can recognize passives, it's easier to remove them from your writing.

To be verb - is/are/was/were/has been/have been/had been/will be/ will have been/being

Exercise: Review your article, identify any passive sentences, and change them to active.

Reduce "there is/are."

Like adverbs and passive language, minimizing there is/are makes your writing stronger. When writing professionally, you need to follow the rules of good writing, so give them a kiss and say goodbye.

Example 1

There are many researchers who believe that TV watching is harmful to kids.

Changed To

Many researchers believe watching TV is harmful to kids.

Example 2

There is one person I love the most.

Changed To

The person I love the most is Sarah.

Exercise 1: Remove there is/there are from the following sentences and rewrite them.

There are going to be hundreds of people attending the conference tomorrow.

There is something that we need to talk about right away.

There is nothing sweet about her.

There are rumors that Tom is having an affair with Stacy.

There is a certainty that only time will tell.

Exercise 2: Review your article for instances of there is/are. Remove them to create stronger sentences.

Remove Redundancies

Are there any extra words in an article you've written recently? Have you said the same thing twice? Sometimes repeating the same ideas in your writing is a part of the strategy or poetic nature of your article, but most of the time, it is unnecessary. Think about how you can accomplish the idea or point without saying it more than once.

Example 1

I was thinking about how great that house was. I was also thinking how great it would be if we had the money to buy it.

I wish we had the money to buy that great house.

In the second sentence, we took out the repetitions or four words and made it a more active sentence.

Example 2

The moon was bright, it was <u>night time</u>, and the <u>sun had recently set.</u>

I soaked in the moonlit sky.

Did you notice that the first sentence tells us that it is set in the evening in three different ways in one sentence? Yikes! Too many words to say the same thing. The second sentence says it once with an active verb. The reader can deduce it is night time.

Exercise 1: Now it's your turn to take one of the sentences you've written that is

repetitive and take out the redundancies.

Replace Stuffy Words with Simpler Ones

At times, we want to show how smart we are by including higher level vocabulary. Now, I'm not saying to dumb down your language; what I'm saying is to make the writing easy to read and relatable.

Example 1

Her egregious and Draconian disposition and superfluous hand gestures made her terrifying to be around.

My stomach knotted when I caught her evil gaze and noticed her wild hand gestures.

Do you see how the first sentence overdoes it a little with the higher-level vocabulary words? The second sentence says the same thing in a way that won't require anyone to crack open their Thesaurus.

Example 2

He had myriad methods for extinguishing vile vermin like this.

He stomped on the rat.

See how the second sentence gets right to the point with a few easy to read words?

Exercise 1: Now, it's your turn. Take some of your purple prose (fancy pants words) and chose easier words. Notice how it changes things for better or worse.

Synonyms

Using synonyms is a great tool for writers. If your article uses the word *child* throughout (depending on the formality of the writing), you might use *kiddo, kid, little one, the fruit of my loins,* and so on. Using synonyms shows your strength as a writer because the writing is more exciting and flows better.

The repetition of the same word bores the reader. Of course, sometimes only one word sums up the noun or point, but think about how
you can use different word forms for that word. For example, if the word is the verb *commissioned,* use the noun *commission*.

Exercise: Choose a few paragraphs of something you've written and find ways to work in some synonyms for words you have re-used too many times.

SECTION 2: Top Grammar Mistakes Even Professional Writers and Bloggers Make

Exercise 1 - Brainstorm what you think the top grammar points are.

Below is a list of the top mistakes. We'll go over each one; then edit your writing to remove them.

Possessives

Possessives are hard to spot and commonly misused. Most people understand that possessives show ownership or belonging; what they don't realize is that only a noun can do the "possessing."

Example 1:

My **mother's car** broke down on the side of the road.

Example 2:

The **dog's bone** fell into the crib from the table.

Example 3:
Another rule to remember is that what follows the possession is a noun, not a verb. You can't own a verb.

Mom's Write should be Moms Write.

Example 4

Another standard error is how apostrophes are used. For a singular noun not ending in -s, you add an apostrophe plus s. Pretty simple. You learned this grade school, but I see this error sometimes.

The **child's toy** fell into the toilet.

Example 5

When a plural noun ends with an "s," simply add an apostrophe to make it possessive.

The **students' grades** were amazing.

When the noun showing the possession is plural, you add the apostrophe after the "s."

But when a plural noun does not end with an "s," add an apostrophe and an "s" to make it possessive.

The **children's toys** littered the room.

Subject-verb Agreements

Subject-verb agreements used to be one of my top writing mistakes. Most of the time, this error is easy to spot, and Microsoft Word will catch it. Other times, the error is harder to notice, so we're covering it now.

Basically, the subject and the verb need to match in number. If the subject is singular, the verb is singular.

Example

The bird is eating the cat's eye.

In the example above, we have one bird, so we use the singular auxiliary verb "is."

If the subject is two birds, as in The birds are eating the cat's eye, we would change the verb *is* to *are*.

Additional Examples

The bird tweets in the early morning light.
The birds tweet in the early morning light.

Pretty simple right? Well, most of the time. But what if you have a more complicated sentence with an unclear subject?

Is the following sentence correct?

Everyone have done the preparation as expected.

No, it isn't correct. "Everyone" is not plural, so the verb needs to be singular.

Everyone has done the preparation as expected.

Is the following sentence correct?

Each of the toys in the room are new.

No, it isn't correct. "Each of the toys" is not plural, so the verb needs to be singular.

Each of the toys in the room is new.

Is the following sentence correct?

The Mayor, as well as his sister, was a guest.

Yes, it is. The subject "The Mayor, as well as his sister," is singular.

Fragments

In English, a complete sentence has a subject and a verb. This sentence is an independent clause that stands on its own, meaning you don't need any additional information to understand it.

I walked to the store.

A fragment either doesn't have a subject or a verb or can't stand on its own; meaning you need additional information to understand the sentence. We can view it as a dependent clause.

Example of Fragments

Although I went there.
Why is it a fragment? Even though the phrase has a subject and verb, it begins with although. Although is a subordinating conjunction and used in dependent clauses. To make the fragment a sentence, you need to add an independent clause.

Although I went there, I forgot the combination to the safe.

In a New York minute.
Why is it a fragment?
The idiomatic phrase, *in a New York minute,* has a lot of meaning but doesn't contain a subject or verb. To make it a complete sentence, you need to add a subject and verb.

In a New York minute, we'll be at our destination.

In San Diego, right before the big intersection.

The fragment above gives us directional information and in spoken English is quite common, but you don't have a verb. Add a verb to complete the sentence.

In San Diego, right before the big intersection, make a left.

<u>*Working far into the night, to complete her homework.*</u>

The fragment above does have a verbal phrase and seemingly a subject, but in fact, the real subject hasn't been mentioned yet. Add a subject to create a complete sentence.

Working far into the night to complete her homework, she tried not to worry about the fact that if she didn't finish it, she would fail the class and get kicked out of school.

Run-on Sentences

A run-on sentence is sentence that goes on forever and ever and doesn't stop, even when you want it to, hope it does, and really would like for the writer to realize that it hasn't stopped. Has it stopped?

When in doubt, break your longer sentences into two. Of course, this depends on your ideas and rhythm, but run-on sentences are bad sentences that can easily be improved with some quick changes.

Claire couldn't stop thinking about Tom and his nerve to kiss her right outside of her boyfriend's house, the night before she was about to have the most important day of her life, the one that would change everything. **RUN-ON SENTENCE**

Claire couldn't stop thinking about Tom. What nerve! He kissed her outside of her boyfriend's mansion, right before the most important day of her life, the day that could quite possibly change everything. **FIXED RUN-ON SENTENCE**

PUNCTUATION

Comma Confusion

Let's be honest, commas are confusing. Where do those little guys go exactly? The purpose of commas is to add a pause between ideas, connect information, and separate the structural information in the sentence.

Some Rules to Guide You

Use a comma to separate two independent clauses connected by *for*, and, nor, but, or and yet. To help you remember, think of the acronym FANBOYS.

Sally stood on top of the car, and Tom balanced the rock on his head.
I would love to travel to the Moon, but I value my life

more.

Introductory transitional phrases need a comma after the dependent clause.

Although he was a clever lad, Claire wrote him off as spoiled and rude.
While Tom guessed he would regret it later, he decided that he would unfriend her on Instagram.

Common starter words for introductory phrases are *although, as, because, while, if, since* and *when*.

Insert a comma when you have a non-essential clause in the sentence.

A non-essential clause isn't necessary for understanding the point or contains nonessential information. It is set off with commas. *Who* and *which* are common relative pronouns used in non-essential clauses.

Claire pointed out Tom to a friend. Tom**, who was wearing his best shirt,** sat in the front row. **Note:** We really don't need to know that he's wearing his best shirt.

Tom's resentment**, which is the main reason for disliking Claire,** bubbled up.

The opposite of a non-essential clause is an essential

clause. An essential clause has important information needed for understanding. These clauses usually begin with *that* and don't need a comma.

Claire loved that Tom despised her. **Having that kind of power** was intoxicating.

In the sentences above, *that* is necessary for complete understanding. The information is essential.

Use a comma when you list items in a sequence.

Tom went to the comic book store, the massage parlor, and the organic grocery store close to his house. He was sure he would run into Claire at each of his stops.

You need a comma when you're listing adjectives to describe a noun.

Tom refused to notice Claire's **thick, blonde, wavy** hair. Note: You need the commas here because we have three adjectives.

Claire's **thick blonde** hair reached her shoulders in sweeping waves. Tom refused to notice. Note: You don't need the comma here because we have two adjectives that coordinate together.

Commas prevent your ideas from becoming confusing.

To Claire, Tom represented everything wrong with men. **Note:** You need the comma to separate the two names; otherwise, the meaning is unclear.

For all of the above reasons, Claire swore off dating for the summer.

Use a comma for dates and geography.

Tom remembered the exact date he had the unfortunate luck to meet Claire -**September 12th, 2017**. He was referring to it as the worst day of his life.

Claire thought Tom was from that podunk town Small Fries, just outside Middle of **Nowhere, Arkansas**. The one known for naked rodeos.

Commas begin quotations and dialogues.

Claire covered her bruised mouth and backed away. **She whispered, "Why** did you kiss me like that for?"
 Tom wasn't sure why, but he was confident he wanted to try it again. "I thought you wanted me to **kiss you," he replied.**

Periods

Periods mark the end of a sentence. You may have been taught to put two spaces after the end of each sentence when you type. The current rule is to use **one space** after periods or ends of sentences.

If you need to fix your piece, use the "find and replace" tool. Click a double space in the find bar and a single space in the replace bar, and your problem will be solved.

Another thing to note if you are writing dialogue is that punctuation like periods is put inside your quotation marks.

Example:

"I'll be five minutes late," she said.

Question Marks and Exclamation Points

Do you have a question? Fine, just don't overuse these!!!

Quotation Marks

Quotation marks are used to quote another person's words. Avoid plagiarism and always give credit.

Example: Melissa Uhles of Pen and Parent said, "I couldn't survive a single day of parenting without my chocolate fix."

Quotation marks are also used for dialogue in novels because there is a character saying something.

Example:

"I'm tired of our teacher hounding us about our grammar mistakes," Sue said.

"I know, and she gets so mad when she sees me start to space out," Jack replied.

Their vs. There

One of the more annoying aspects of the English language is homophones. Homophones are words that have the same sound and pronunciation but have different meanings.

New vs. Knew
Write vs. Right
Their vs. There vs. They're

Their is a possessive pronoun or determiner. You use it to show ownership, reference something mentioned before, and in titles. *Their* can be singular or plural and used to reference either sex.

Their plane takes off in twenty minutes for Cancun.
I offered to watch *their* house while they were gone.

Their is typically followed by a noun.

There, on the other hand, is easily confused with *their* and has more uses. It can be a noun, adjective, or adverb.

We walked from *there* to *there* in one afternoon. NOUN
My husband noted that *there* was a man lurking around the playground. ADJECTIVE

Note: I'm breaking my own rule by using that there in a sentence. It's being used as a teaching example. I would further rewrite this sentence as, "My husband noted a man was lurking around the playground."

I want to go over *there*. ADVERB

Vague Pronoun Reference

Every pronoun you write should refer clearly to a noun. The noun is called the antecedent.

Example 1
After buying some **chips**, she crammed **them** down.
The pronoun *them*, clearly refers to the noun *chips*.

Example 2
Tom bought **chocolate** and gave **it** to Claire.
The pronoun **it** clearly refers to the noun **chocolate**.

But sometimes the connection between the pronoun and the antecedent is vague.

Example 1

We decided to take the **<u>tires and seats</u>** out of the car and fix **<u>them.</u>**

In the case above, the antecedent *them* could refer to either *tires or seats*. To fix this problem, you'd replace *them* with a noun.

We decided to take the tires and seats out of the car and fix **<u>the tires.</u>**

Example 2
If Tom doesn't come on time and with chocolate, she'll never forgive him for it.
We aren't sure if she'll never forgive him for not coming on time or for not bringing chocolate or both. To fix this, you can replace *it* with a noun or rewrite the sentence.

Revision 1 If Tom doesn't come on time and with chocolate, she'll never forgive him for being late and empty-handed.

Revision 2
Claire decided that if Tom's late and empty-handed, she'll never forgive him for either.

OR just ...she'll never forgive him.

One way to spot a vague pronoun reference is to look for the use of *it* in your sentences. But *which* and *that* can cause problems as well.

Example 3
Sophia always failed her exams, which made them very unhappy.

Revision
Sophia always failed her exams; making her teachers unhappy.

A misplaced or dangling modifier

A modifier adds or gives extra information about the noun. It can be an adjective, adverb, or phrase. A misplaced modifier might not be next to the noun it modifies, and this placement may confuse the reader. You need to tighten up your sentence by moving the dangling modifier closer to the noun.

Misplaced Adjective Modifier

Example 1
The man ate a warm dish of mush for lunch.

In the sentence, we aren't sure if the man ate a warm dish or warm mush.

Revision
The man ate warm mush for lunch.

Now, that we moved the *modifier adjective warm,* closer to *mush* the sentence meaning is clear.

Example 2
The plastic man's hairbrush fell to the floor.
In the sentence, we aren't sure if the man is plastic or his hairbrush.

Revision
The man's plastic hairbrush fell to the floor.

Now, that we moved the *modifier adjective plastic,* closer to hair brush the sentence meaning is clear.

Misplaced Adverb Modifier

Example
Tom and Claire stared while they ate longingly.

In the sentence, we aren't sure whether Tom and Claire *ate longingly* or *stared longingly.*

Revision

Tom and Claire stared longingly at each other as they ate.

Now, that we moved the *modifier adverb longingly,* closer to *stared* the sentence meaning is clear.

Misplaced phrase

Tom and Claire bought a house of red bricks.
In the sentence, we aren't sure whether Tom and Claire bought a house of red bricks or a red brick house.

Revision

Tom and Claire bought a red brick house.

Now, the meaning is clear.

Example 2

Three comedians ate handfuls of popcorn sitting quietly in the corner.

Revision

Three comedians sat quietly in the corner, eating handfuls of popcorn.

That wraps up Grammar for Writers & Bloggers! I know that by becoming a grammar and syntax expert, you'll be a more sought-after writer and blogger. Also, now you can be that annoying person that goes on Facebook and corrects everyone else's grammar. Just kidding, don't do that.

With these tools, you'll have more confidence when it comes time to pitch your blog posts. Even if you end up using editors, they will be thrilled that you have the basics down. Not only that, you'll craft better posts for your own blog and brand.

BONUSES

Identify Your Tells

When receiving feedback on your writing, one of the most common comments is "show, don't tell." Receiving such a comment may be confusing because this slip is hard to notice. And sometimes you need to get right to the point.

But "showing" instead of "telling" draws the reader in and makes your words vivid and emotional. Nothing is worse than being "told" what to do or feel. Believe me, I've tried this with my toddler.

We want the writing to lead us down a path to some understanding or transformation. Your creative endeavors are not about what you want, but rather what the reader deserves.

However, many writers write first for themselves, without considering the audience, and then might, in their editing process, begin to shape the writing for the reader. For some writers, overthinking about who is going to read their work blocks their creativity. So, write for yourself than for others.

Example 1 - Telling

He said goodbye angrily.

Changed to Showing

He slammed the phone down on the table.

In the above example, we know the man is angry because he slammed the phone down. People usually only take this action when they are mad or upset.

Example 2 - Telling

He glanced at her forehead. She's angry, he thought.

Changed to Showing

He glanced at the vein bulging on her otherwise smooth forehead.

We know she's angry because of the vein bulging on her forehead.

Exercise 1: Write a paragraph inspired by the sentence, "She is sad." First, brainstorm words you can use instead of "sad." Afterward, write a paragraph showing us why she's sad.

Use Descriptive Senses

Describing the scene using the senses will encourage *showing* rather than *telling*. The sense used the most is sight, but don't limit yourself to one sense.

The five senses include sight, taste, touch, hearing, and feeling.

In your writing, you don't have to use all of the senses at once, but choosing to use one or two makes your writing more interesting and alive. Choose details that are relevant and needed for the story and skip the rest. If you go into too much detail, you'll bore your reader.

Let's look at a few examples of using the senses to show rather than to tell.

Telling Statement
He was embarrassed.

Showing with Sight & Feeling
The red sting of embarrassment spread across his chubby cheeks.

Telling Statement
She listened to the birds.

Showing with Sound
Leaning back against the cold bench, she allowed the early morning chatter of the blue jays to soothe her bruised heart.

Exercise 2: Go to a coffee shop, playground, park, or children's bedroom, and list adjectives/nouns to describe the scene for each of the senses. Use a thesaurus, if needed.

Once you make a list of descriptive words to describe the scene in the coffee shop or your home, write a paragraph of 5-8 sentences.

Exercise 3: Review the article you're writing and identify your tells. Change your *tells* to *shows* by using the senses.

Reduce Adverbs

Mentioning adverbs in the context of showing rather than telling is essential. Adverbs add or modify the verb or adjectives in the sentence, so if you include them, you're giving more telling information, rather than showing.

Example *with* **Adverb**
I streaked proudly down the street.

Example *without* **Adverb**
I streaked down the busy street, remembering the days of skinny dipping at the pond.

Example *with* **Adverb**
She mightily bit a cream cheese slathered bagel.
Example *without* **Adverb**
She bit a cream cheese slathered bagel.

Exercise 1: Review your writing again for your adverb use and remove any that aren't needed.

Use Dialogue

Using dialogue is a useful technique for reducing tells in your writing. When characters speak, you show through dialogue. Some writers use dialogue in several pages, while others have a few choice sentences of dialogue.

Without Dialogue

He was embarrassed. He glanced at her red face. Perhaps, she would change her mind. After all, she was the one who had suggested it years before. He leaned back heavily against the cold bench. The birds chirped madly.

With Dialogue

"Do you remember when we came here last?" he asked.

She swept the hair out of her eyes and hesitated. "No," she replied.

But he wasn't sure if he believed her. It was now or never, he thought.

"I think it's time we killed her." There, he had said it. He leaned back against the cold bench and waited.

The only sign she had heard him was the flush of red creeping up her pale cheeks. Of course, it could be the cold morning air, but he suspected otherwise.

"No," she said. "It's too late for that."

"But, you're the one who suggested it," he whispered. Even out in the woods, away from the main house where she slept, he was afraid someone would hear them. The only response was the mad chirping of the blue jays.

Exercise 1: Write a paragraph without dialogue and with dialogue for the following writing prompt.

Describe the Best or Worst Day of Your Life

Exercise 2: Review your article. Can you insert dialogue for a telling passage?

Use Big Fat Nouns

Big fat nouns are nouns that are more descriptive without having to use adjectives. Instead of using *house,* you could use *mansion, shack, townhouse, duplex, ranch house, cottage* and so on. Being specific with nouns to describe the scene will add clarity and depth to your writing.

Exercise 1: Read the following paragraph, underline the nouns and then replace them with big fat nouns. Use a thesaurus, if necessary. Reread the paragraph out loud.

She strolled along the street. After a bit, she decided to stop at the store. Once inside, she made her way to the aisle with the sleeping aids. Looking around, she reminded herself that no one had followed her. As a newcomer to this town, no-one knew her. But still, her ears burned. At the end of the aisle, next to the cleaning products, a man stared.

Exercise 2: Review something you've written. What simple nouns can you replace with

big fat nouns?

Use Metaphors

"And your very flesh shall be a great poem."

Walt Whitman

Using metaphors is another tool to reduce *tells* in your

writing. Metaphors enliven your writing with a minimum number of words and brighten the imagination of your readers. They also create new meaning and showcase your writing talent.

I think of how a child sees the world when I contemplate metaphors. When a child looks into the foliage and sees a monkey dancing on the leaves, though it's only the wind ruffling the edges, he's using a metaphor.

When your husband holds up the almost empty pot of coffee and asks, "How many cups have you had?" And you respond with, "Two, but they are usually made up of the bottom of the barrel," you are using a metaphor.

Metaphor is when you compare two things and make them alike without using *like* or *as*. If you use *like* or *as*, then this is a simile, not a metaphor. Metaphors are common in poetry and literature but can add color to any type of writing, including blog posts.

He smiles **like** a cat with a bottomless pot of cream. *Simile*

His smile resembles a cat with a bottomless pot of cream. **Metaphor.**

Sometimes certain metaphors become common phrases in everyday life, making them cliched when used in your writing.

He needed to **tie up loose ends.**

It's **crystal clear** to me.

Thomas is a **couch potato.**

Metaphors are figurative language, and sometimes your creative brain needs some help
to generate them. The following exercise should help you reach the creative depths of your soul (yes, metaphor intended).

Exercise 1: Do you remember Mad Libs? Try making up some incomplete sentences. Come back later and fill in the blanks with different parts of speech. Or if you prefer, work on this project with a partner or kiddo. Don't overthink it.

Exercise 2: Make a list of ten people you know. Create a metaphor to represent their personalities or habits. For example, *if the person is a co-worker you don't trust, you might say, He's a rat. Or I wouldn't trust him with a ten-foot pole.*

Exercise 3: Review the article you wrote. Have you used a metaphor? If so, is it cliched or boring? If not, are there any other areas where you could use metaphor effectively?

Reduce Prepositions

I'm sure you're gathering the theme of good writing/blogging - less is more. Well, this concept applies to prepositions as well. Some examples of prepositions are: with, at, in, on, about, around, and so on. Prepositions connect ideas, describe the position of something or when it happens.

They describe, for example:

Position of something:

The pen is <u>on</u> the table.

The time something happens:

The party will begin <u>at</u> 9 o'clock.

How something happens:

We usually go <u>by</u> bus to see the parade.

Prepositions can be more than one word.

The woman sat down <u>next to</u> me on the train, and I forgot my name.

How do you reduce prepositions?

Use the active voice

Delete prepositional phrases

Use the genitive or possessive

Eliminate nominalizations

Now, let's go over each way in more detail.

Use the active voice

We covered this in a previous unit, but it's essential to review.

By using the active voice, not only will your writing be stronger, but you'll also reduce prepositions.

Passive Sentence
Warm milk is added **to** the bread **by** the baker.

Active Sentence
The baker adds warm milk **to** the bread.

You reduced the number of adverbs from two to one.

Delete prepositional phrases

Prepositional phrases include a preposition + adjective + noun

in the warm water
next to the flickering light
on the pink chair

You have to decide if this prepositional phrase is necessary.

Sentence with the prepositional phrase
The boat will be waiting in the warm water at 10 o'clock.

Sentence without the prepositional phrase
The boat will be waiting at 10 o'clock.

Sentence with the prepositional phrase
Tim found a small nail next to the flickering light and put it in his pocket.

Sentence without the prepositional phrase
Tim found a small nail and put it in his pocket.

Use the genitive or possessive

Using the genitive or possessive will help reduce prepositions. The possessive means that the noun owns something.

Examples of possession

My mother**'s purse** fell into the water.

The children**'s** mother**'s purse** fell into the dirty bay water.

Reducing prepositions by using the possessive.

She was relieved by the desire of the children to go to sleep.

The children's desire to sleep gave her a sense of relief.

The t-shirt of the muses slipped from her pale shoulders.

The muse's t-shirt slipped from her pale shoulders.

Eliminate nominalizations

Nominalizations are buried or smothered verbs. Uncovering these verbs will add clarity to your writing.

Sentence with nominalization
Their need for justifying of why they went to the beach was unnecessary.

Sentence without nominalization
They didn't need to justify going to the beach.

You eliminated four words, two of them prepositions.

Exercise 1: Count the number of words in an article/blog you wrote recently. Rewrite your article to have 300 fewer words. To reduce prepositions, look for instances where you can change passive to active, delete prepositional phrases, and eliminate nominalizations.

Quick Grammar Checklist

Are you about to press *send* or hit *publish*? Wait! Take a look at your writing one more time. Did you clear up the following issues? Once you do, you'll be a polished writing super-star!

Are you using possessives correctly?

Is the subject-verb agreement working?

Do you have any fragments that need to become full sentences?

Are there any painfully long run-on sentences?

Does your piece use their, there and they're in the right way?

Do you need to fix any vague pronoun references?

Can you spot a misplaced or dangling modifier?

Is there a way to reduce the adverbs in your writing?

Is there any way to cut the word *that*?

Have you shown an excellent variety in your sentences?

Are you using parallel structure?

Are there too many instances of is/are in your piece?

If you've said something twice, can you remove redundancies?

Have you replaced *stuffy words* with simpler ones?

Have you had a chance to have fun using synonyms?

Can you be less passive and use stronger verbs? *See our power verbs sheet.*

Did you run a spell check and use <u>Grammarly</u> to spot

errors you may have missed?

Powerful Verbs

Abstain

Aggravate

Attack

Baste

Bolster

Brood

Cajole

Capture

Claw

Determine

Devour

Dig

Endanger

Envelop

Escalate

Fight

Forage

Fashion

Garble

Grasp

Grimace

Hurry

Hug

Hyperventilate

Incite

Instruct

Joke

Jostle

Justify

Kickbox

Kid

Kill

Lean

Lift

Litigate

Mock

Murder

Mystify

Nestle

Nod

Nosh

Obliterate

Order

Officiate

Paralyze

Perceive

Punish

Question

Quit

Quote

Rally

Recoil

Squeeze

Sprinkle

Steer

Taste

Tear

Toddle

Understand

Unearth

Uproot

Vacillate

Vacuum

Veer

Wash

Withdraw

Whistle

Wrestle

Yawn

Yearn

Yell

Zip

Write down your favorite power verbs.

Keep learning with our other books for writers:

Write Compelling Content

How to Make a Living as a Writer

Find tons of FREE resources at Pen and Parent

If you enjoyed this book, we'd be super grateful if you'd leave us a

review on the site where you purchased it.

Happy Writing!

Made in the USA
Coppell, TX
20 May 2020